Animals Coloring Book

PSYCHEDELIC STRESS-RELIEVING ANIMALS

A Coloring Book For Adults

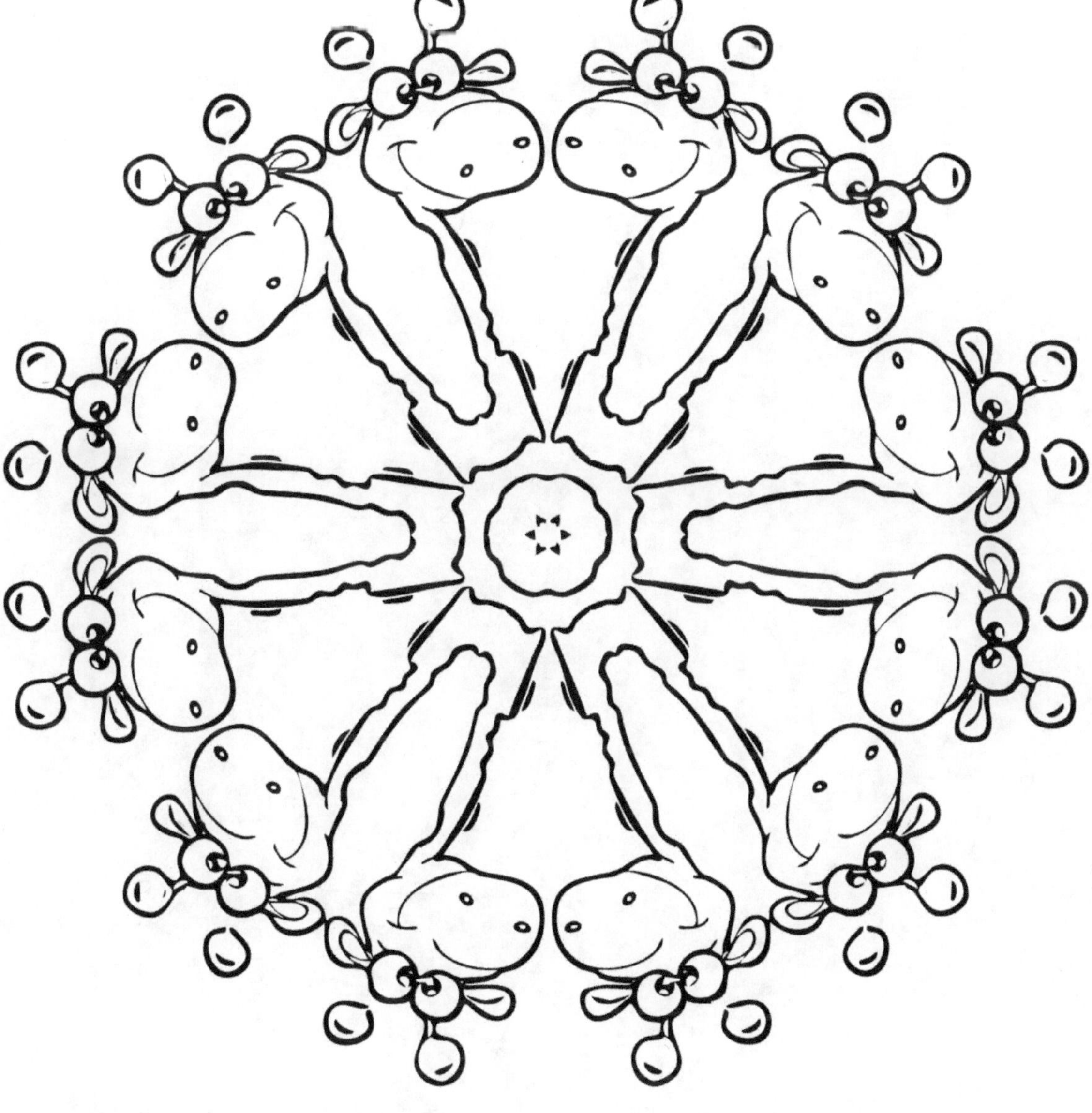

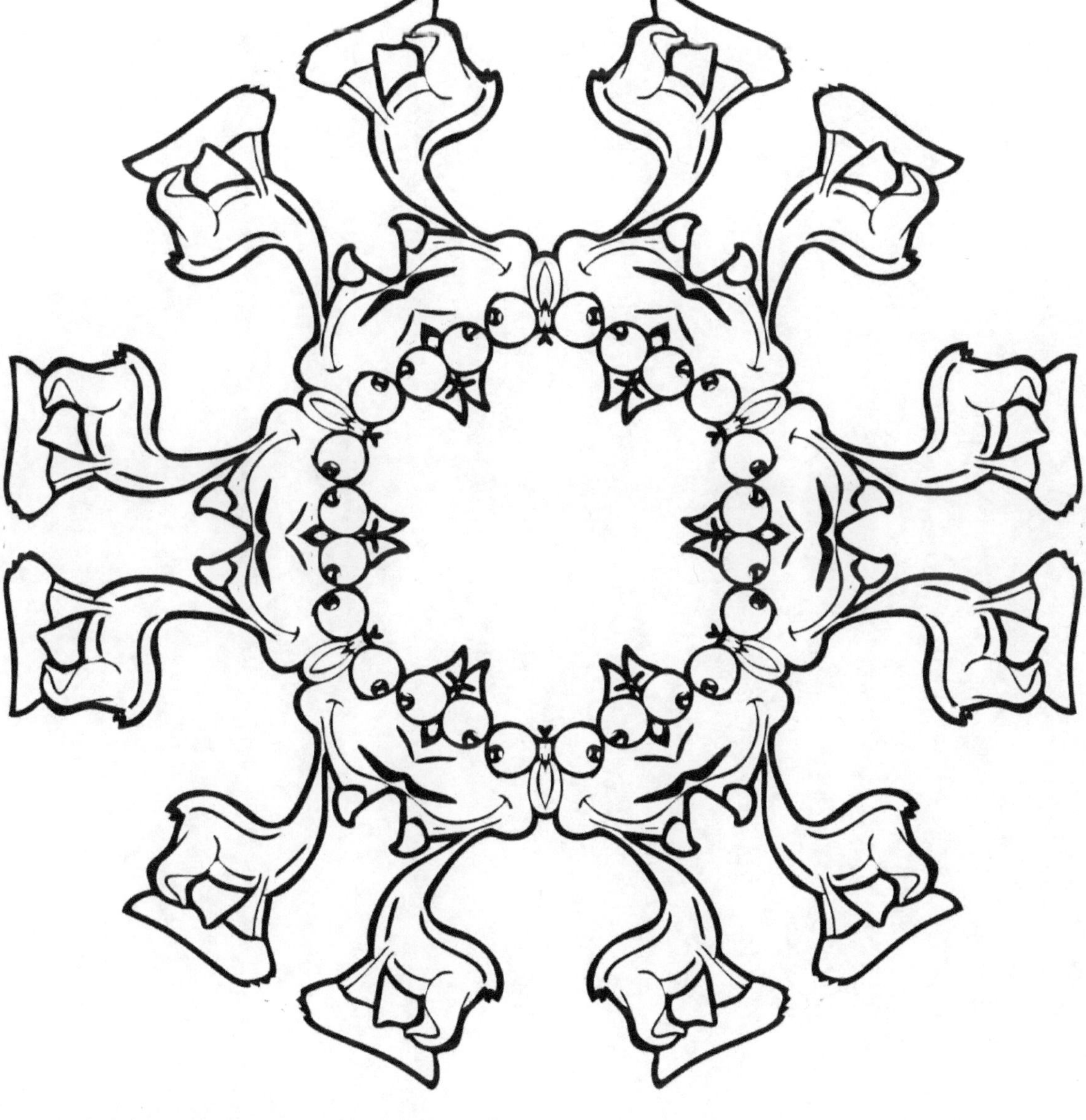

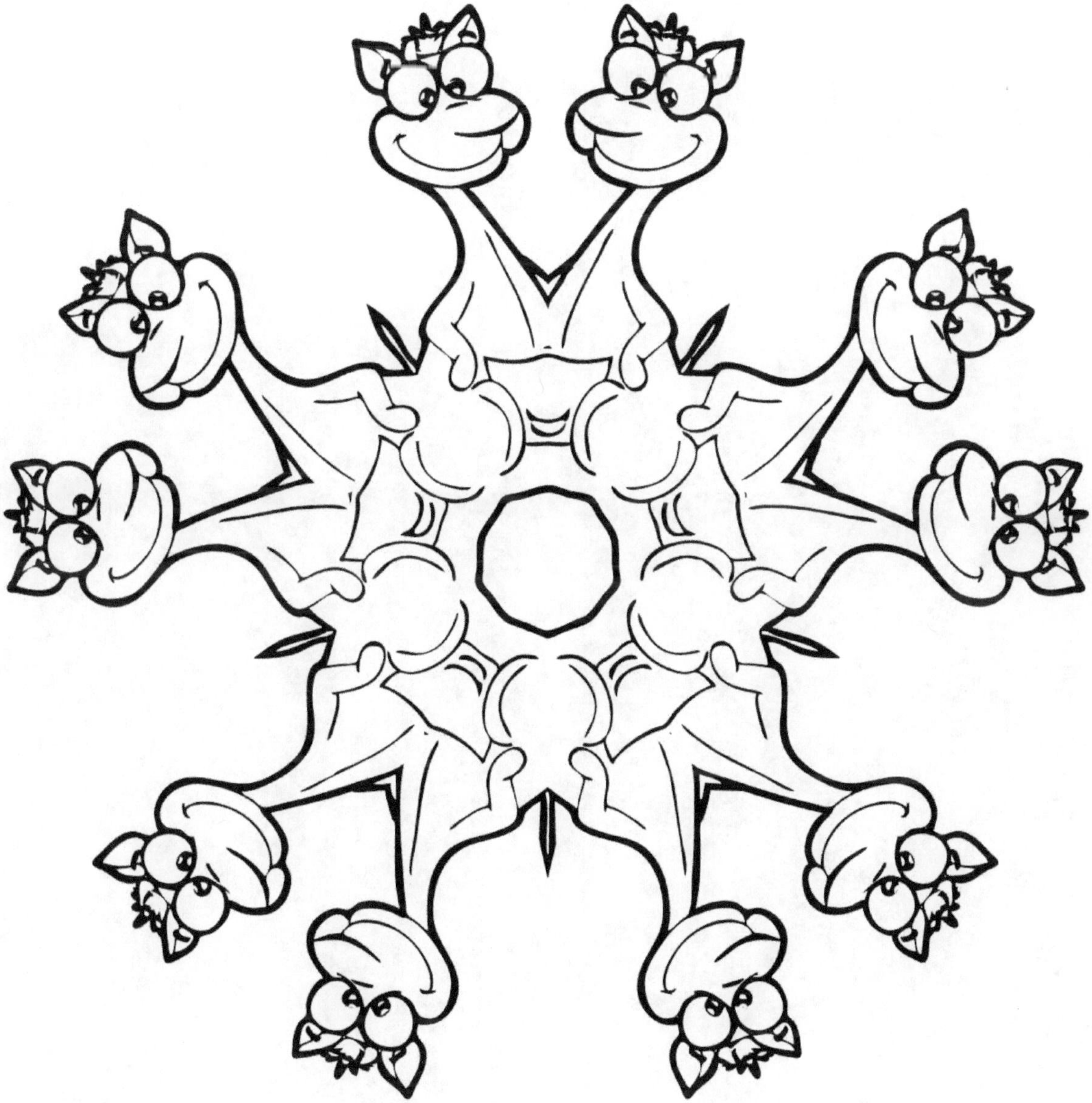

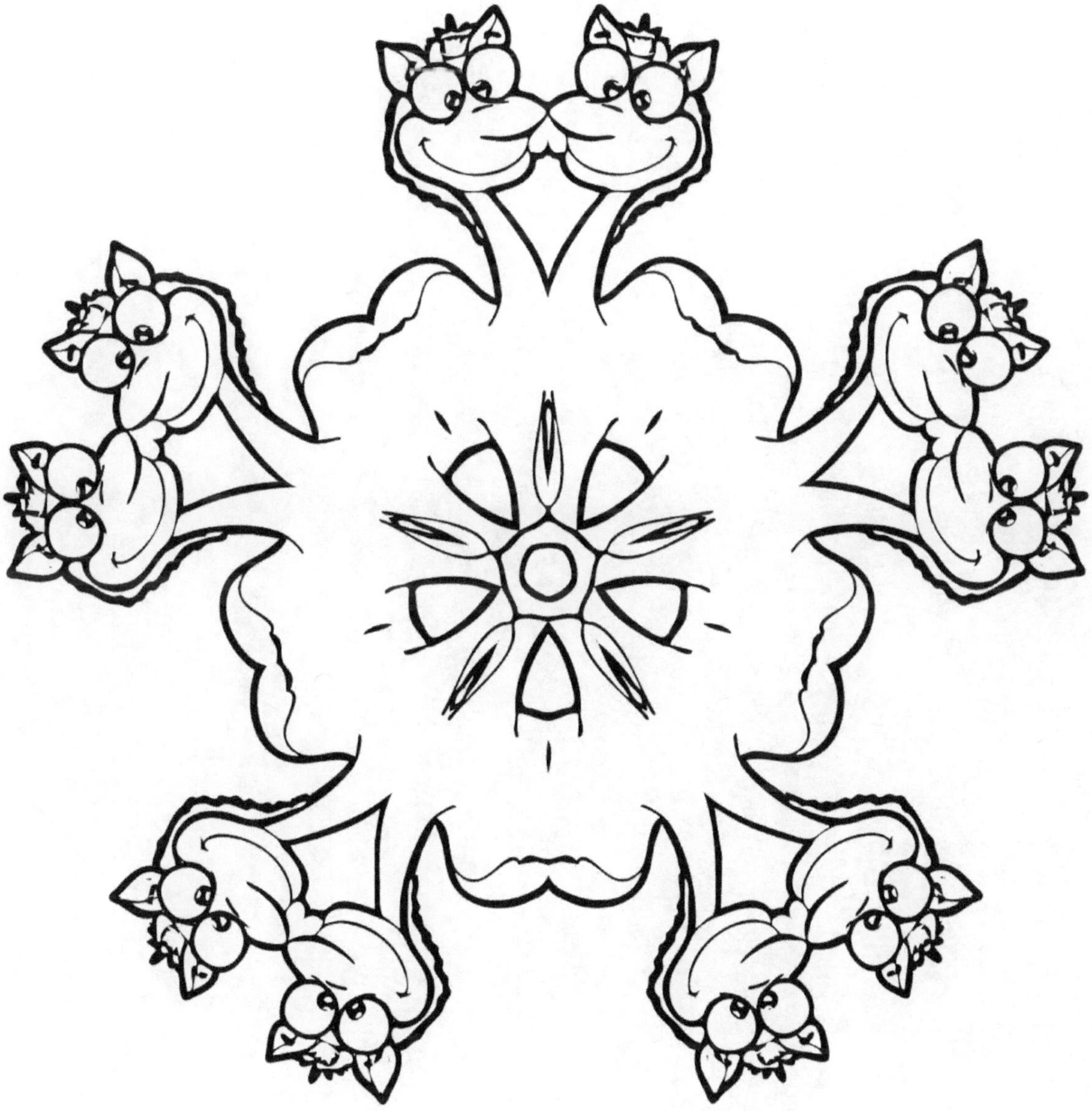

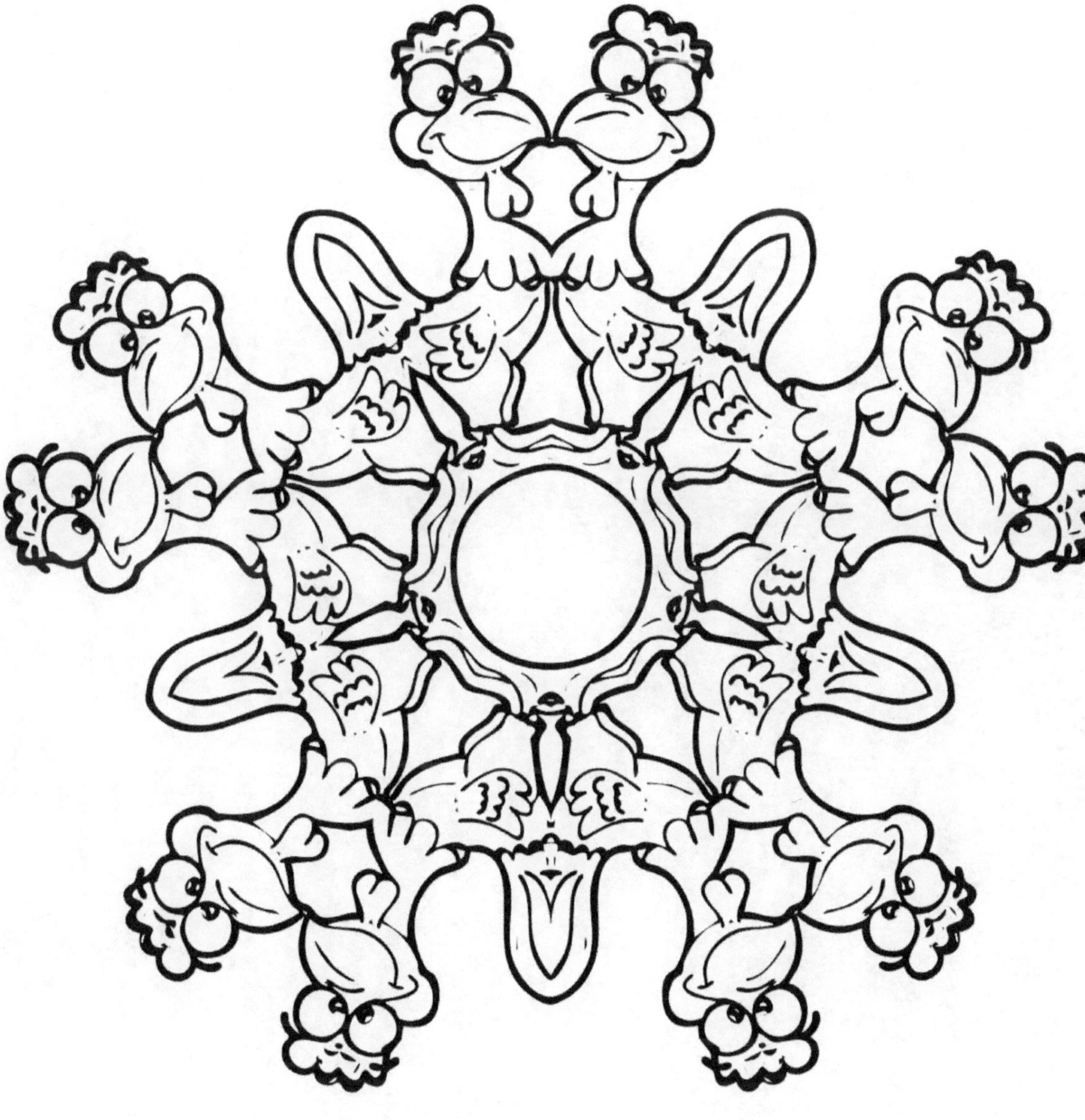

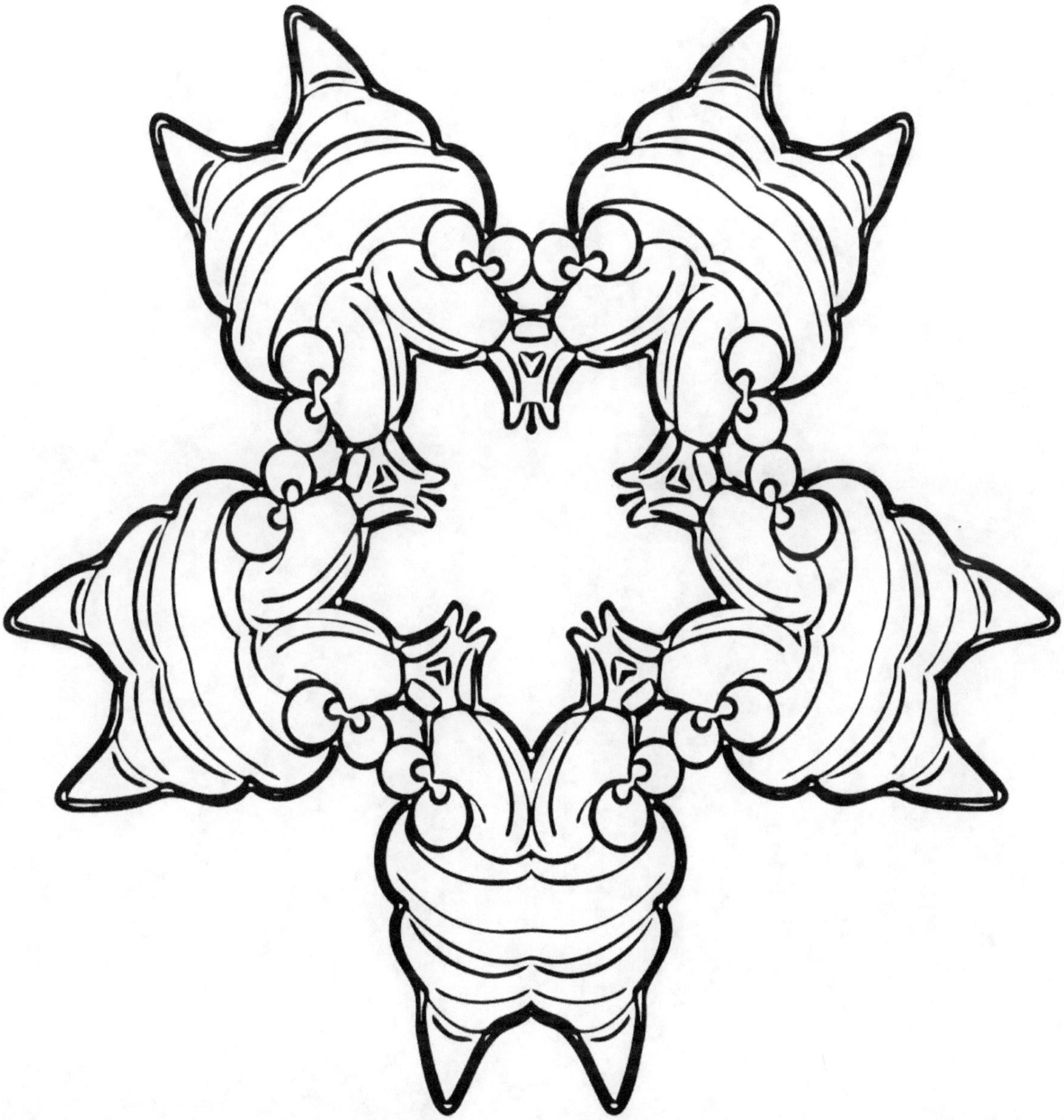

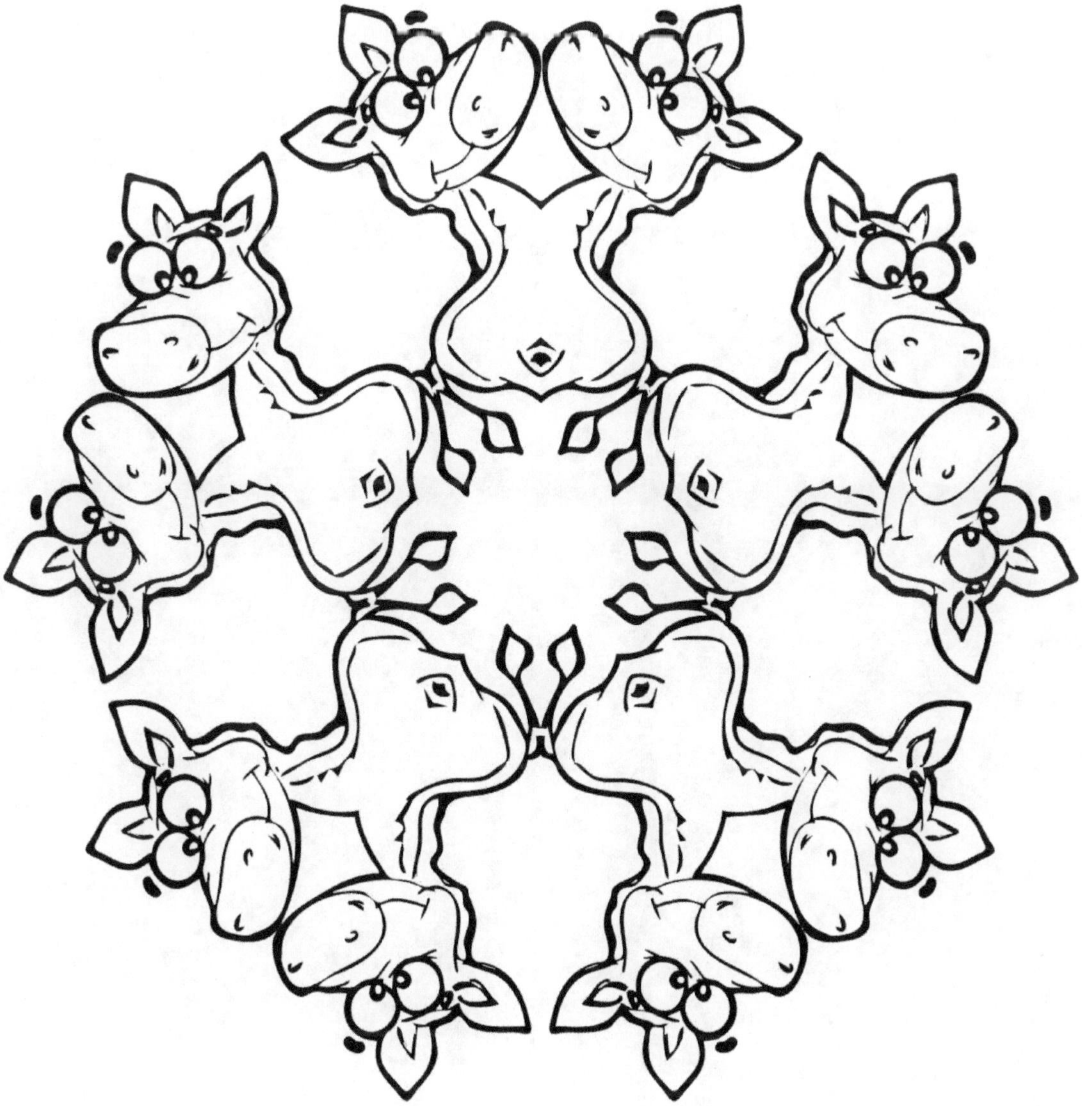

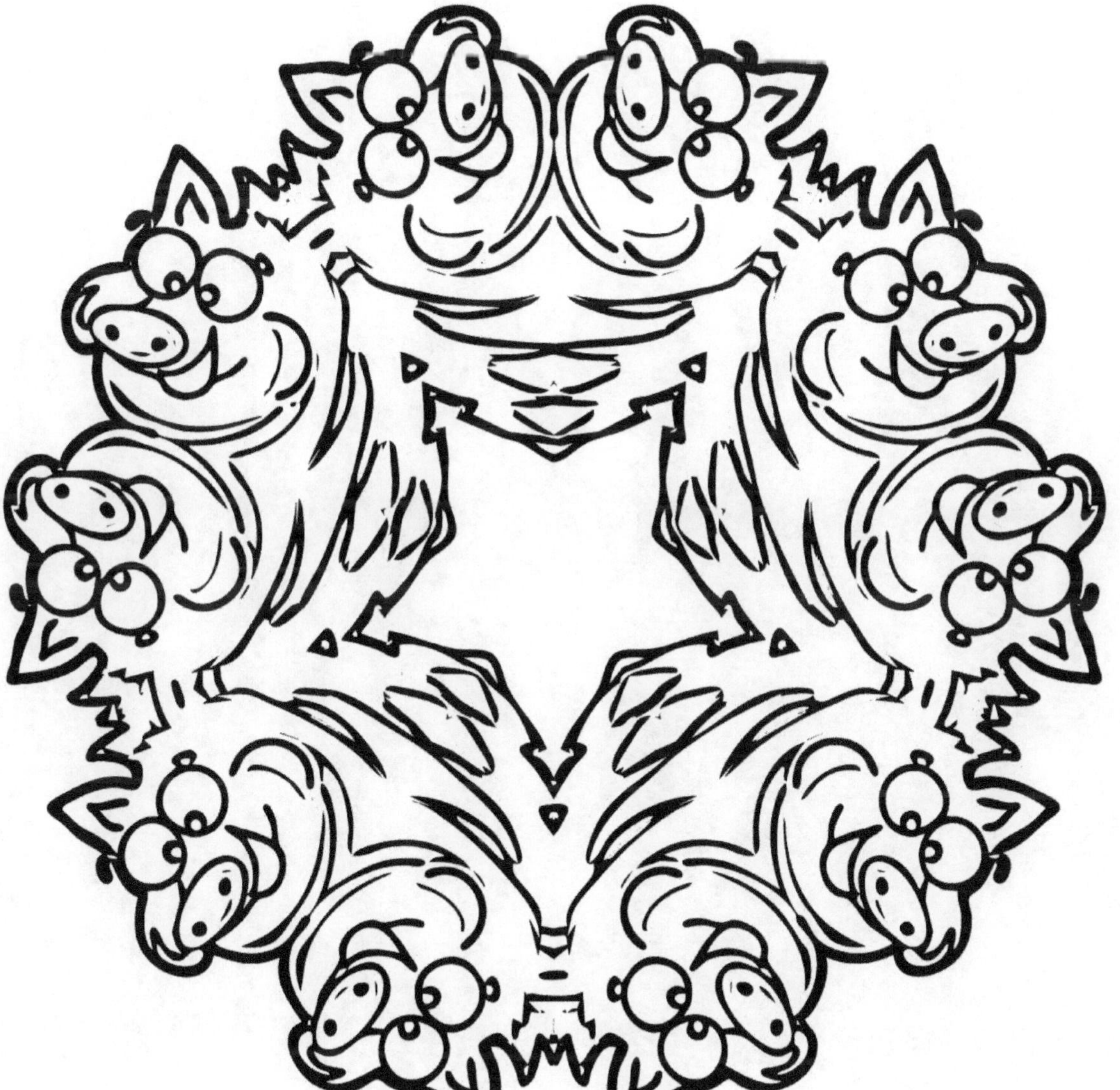

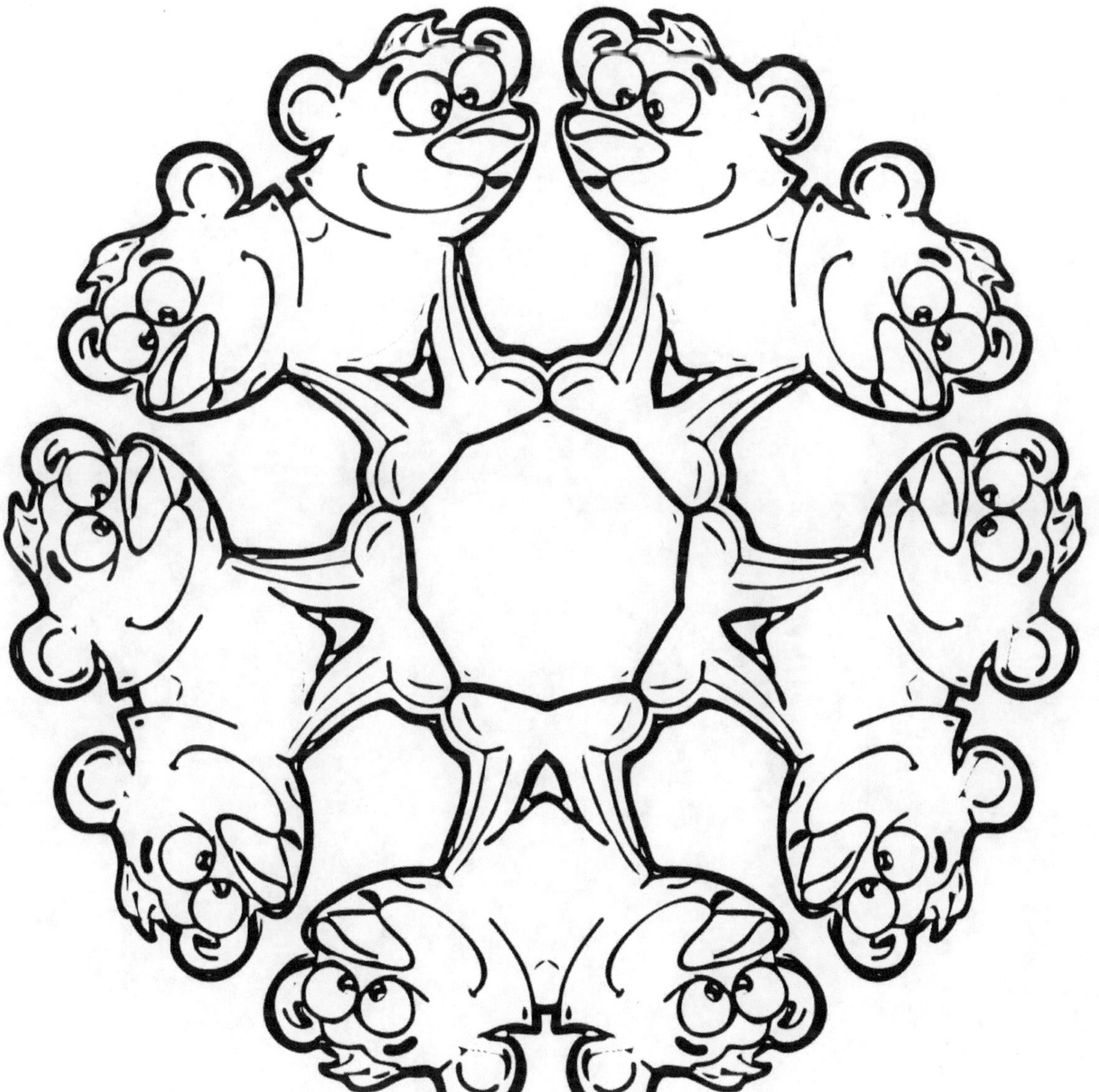

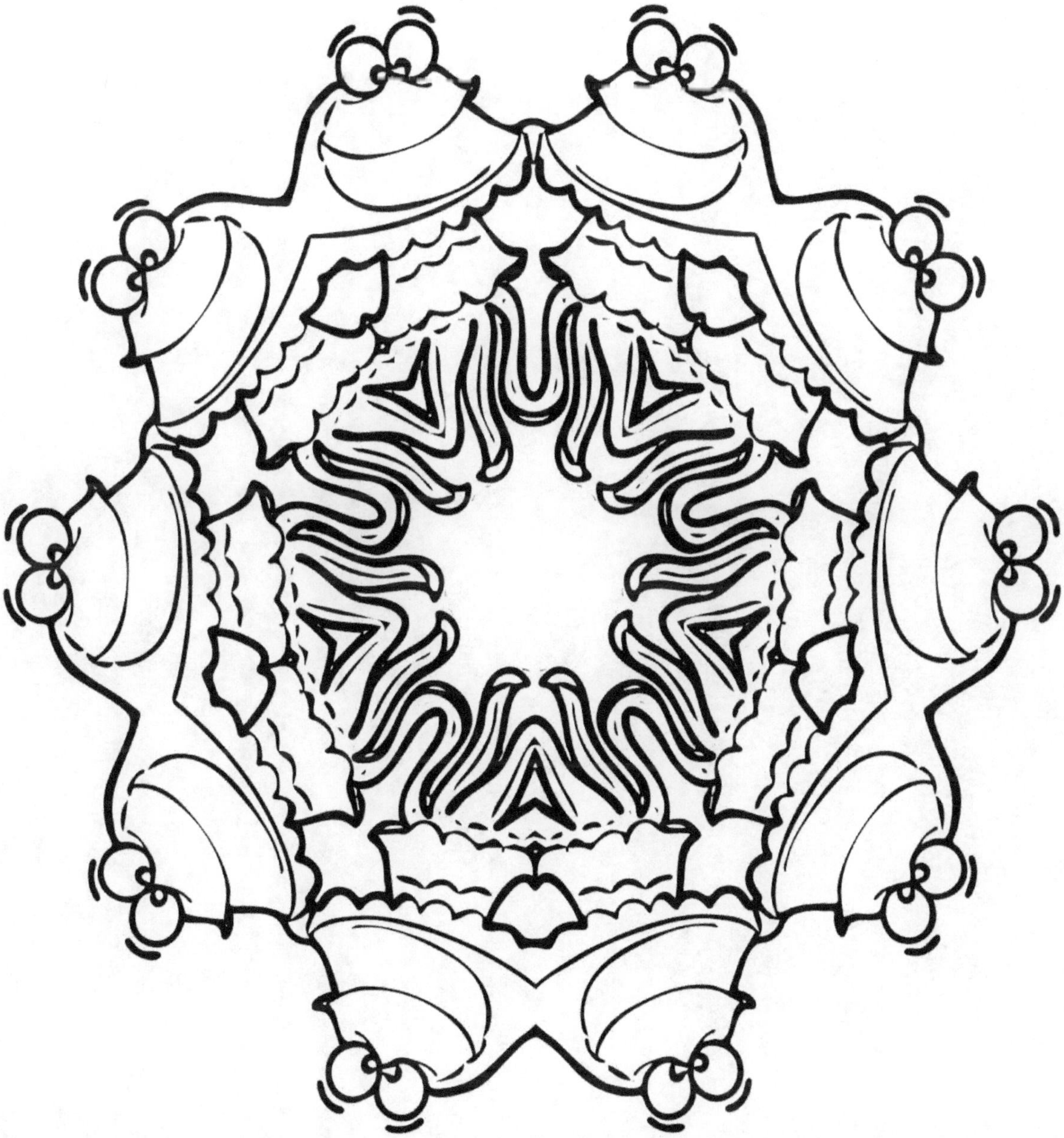

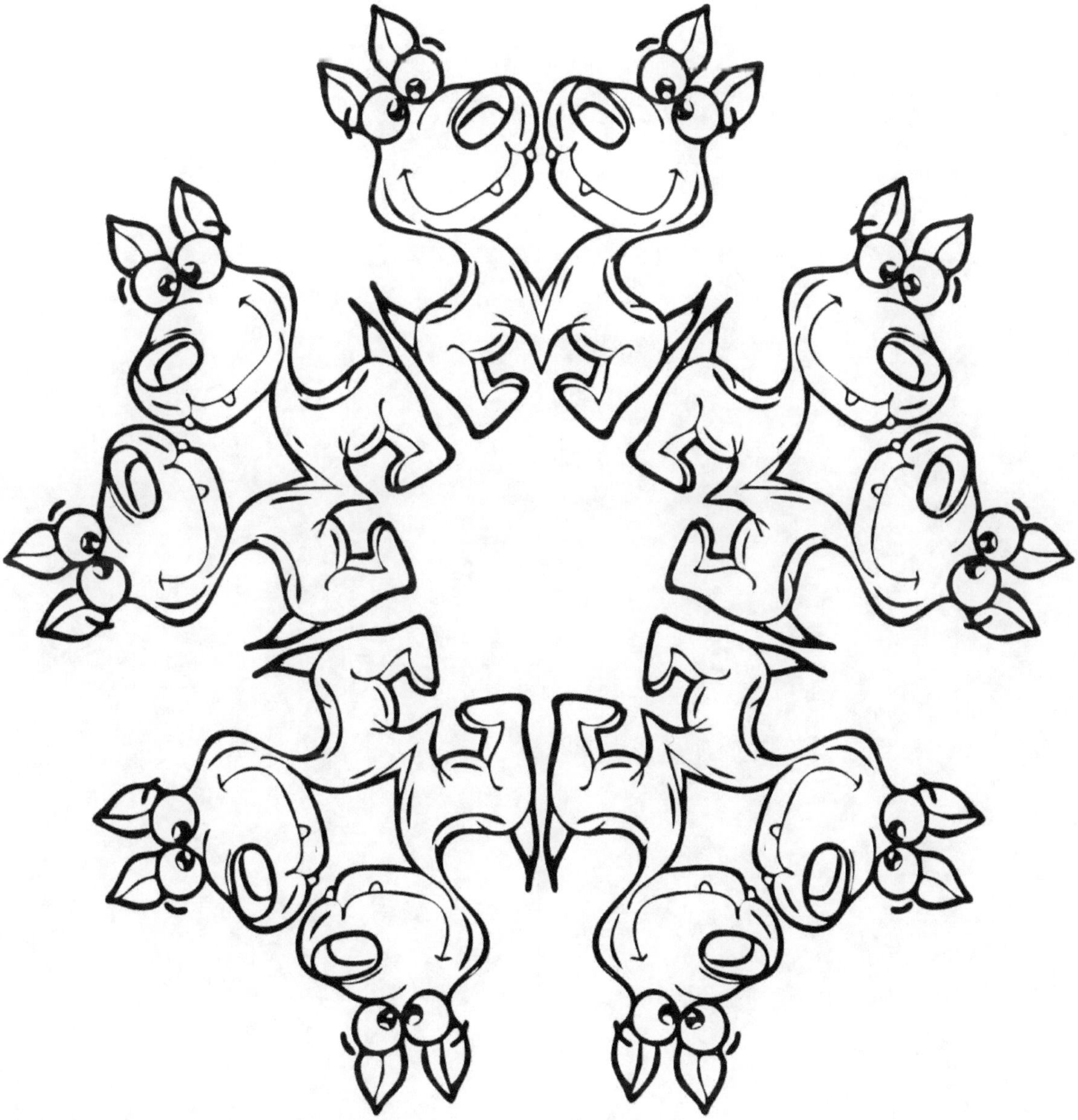

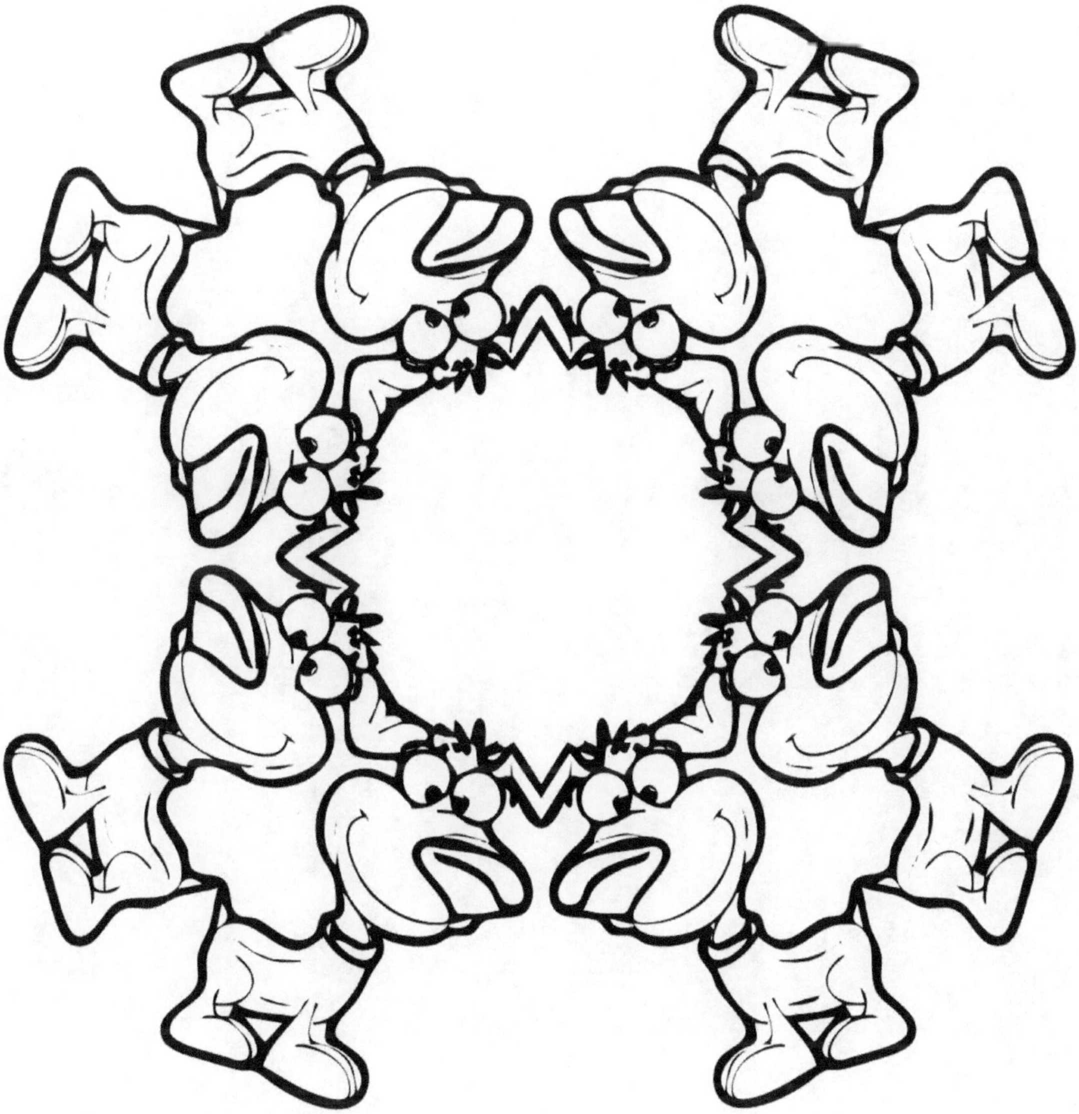

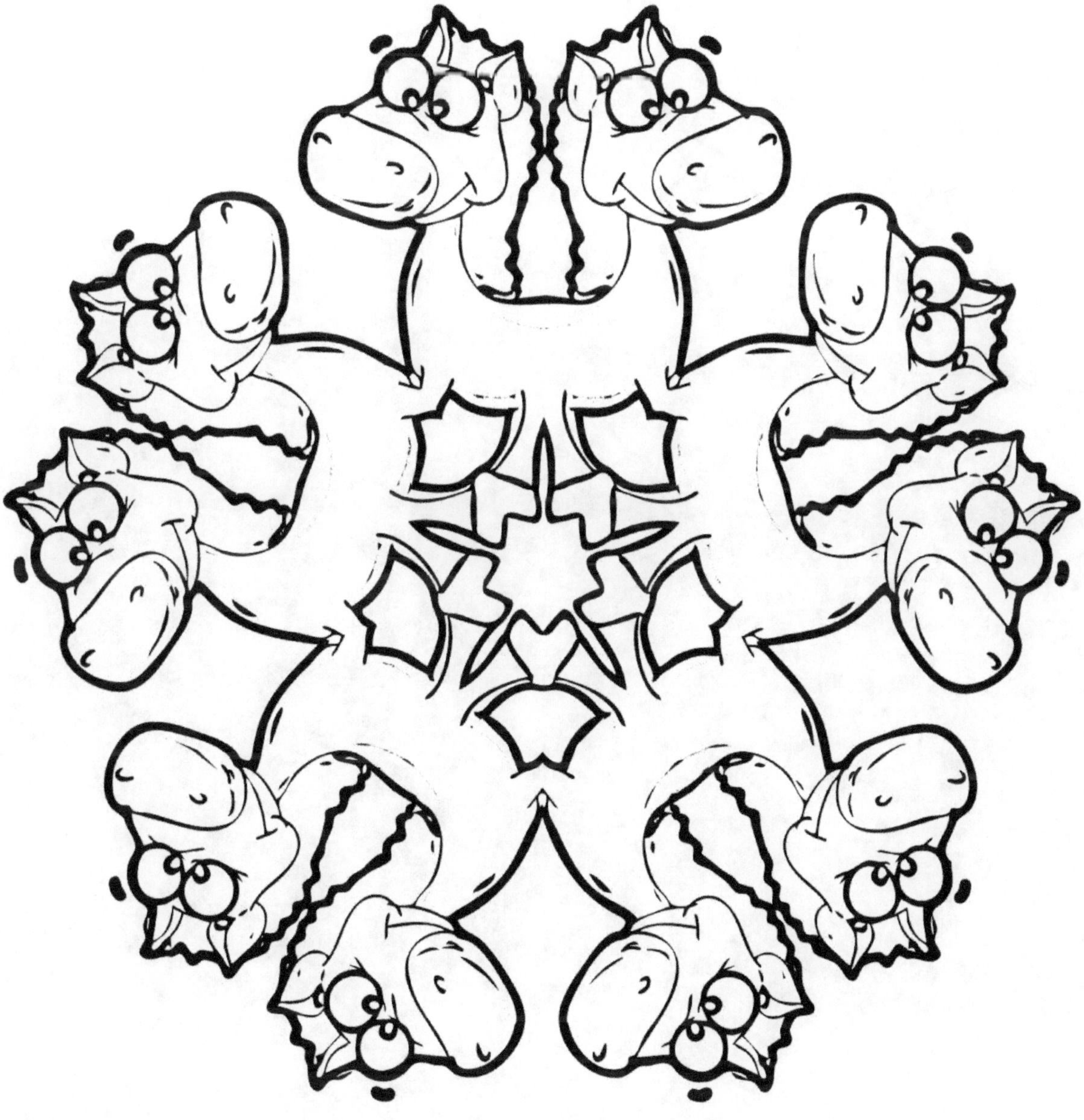

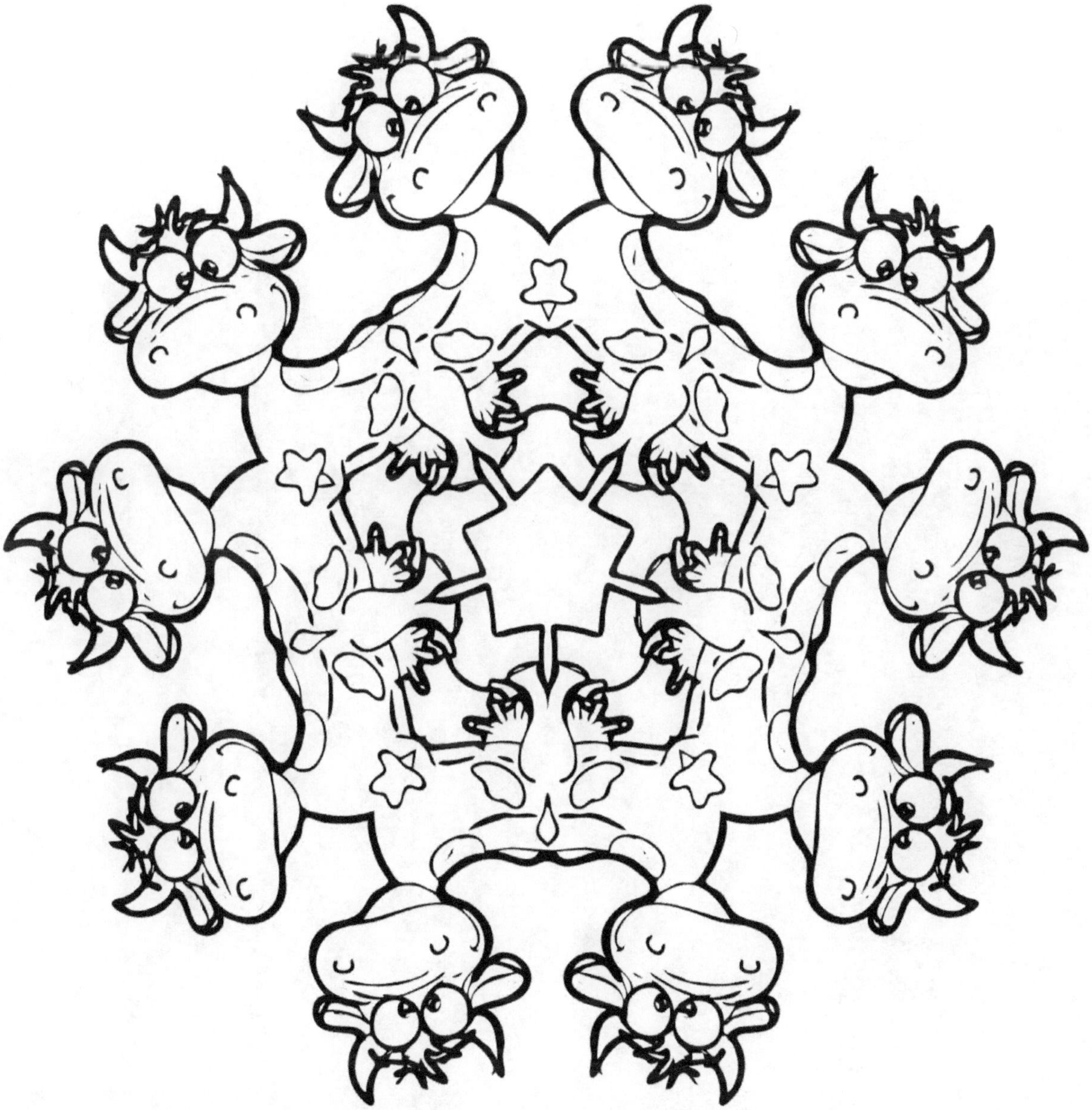

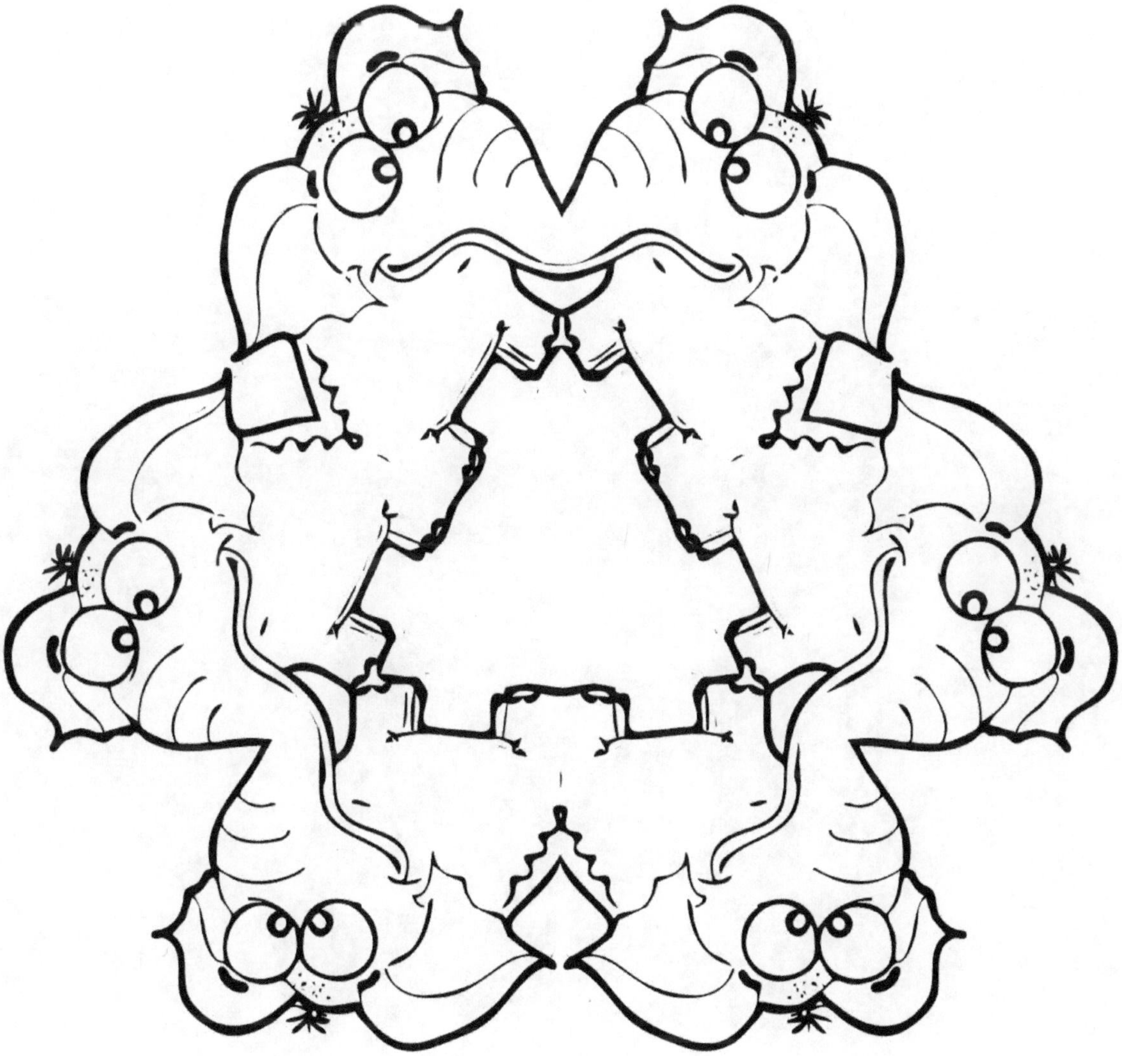

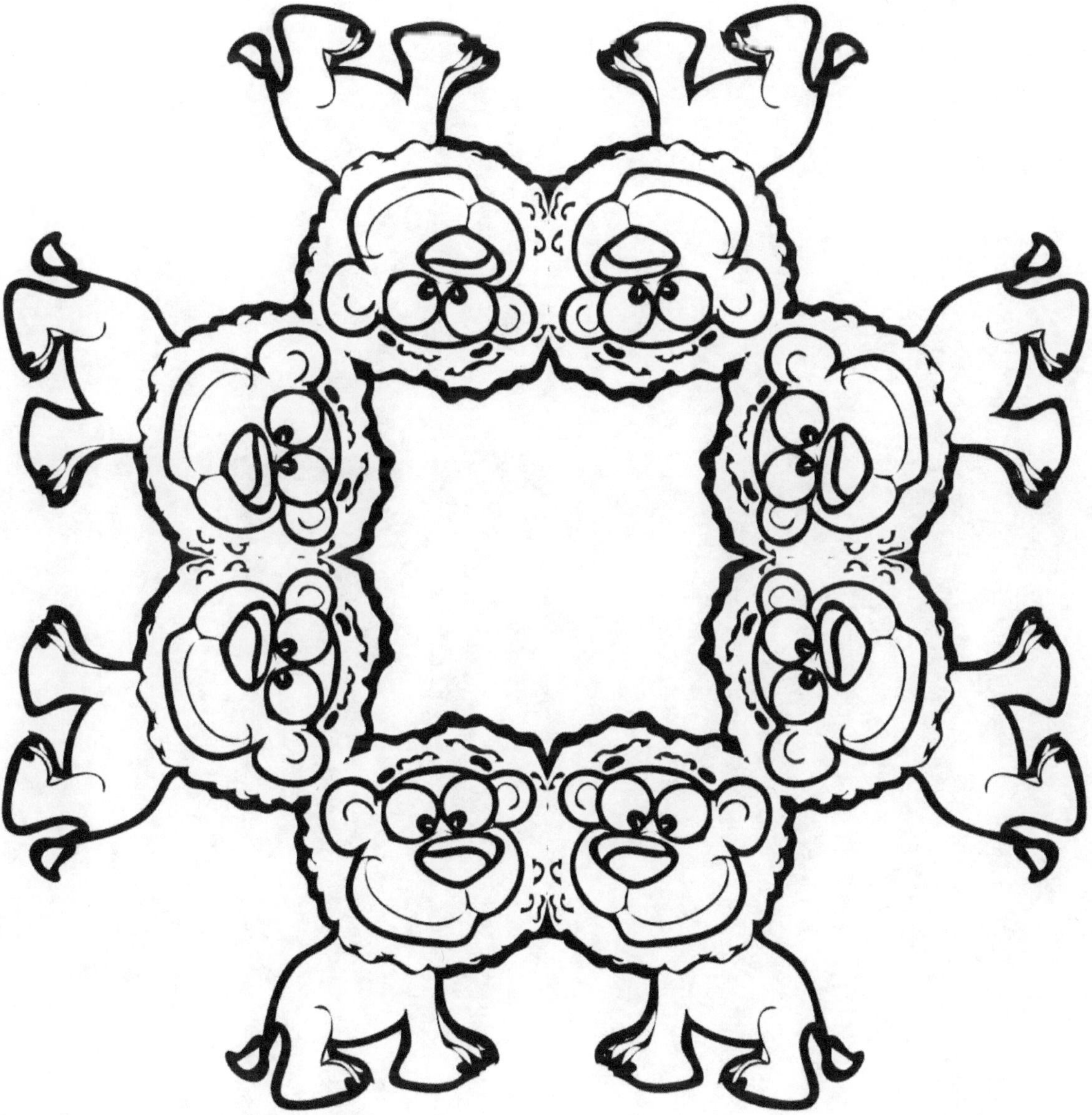

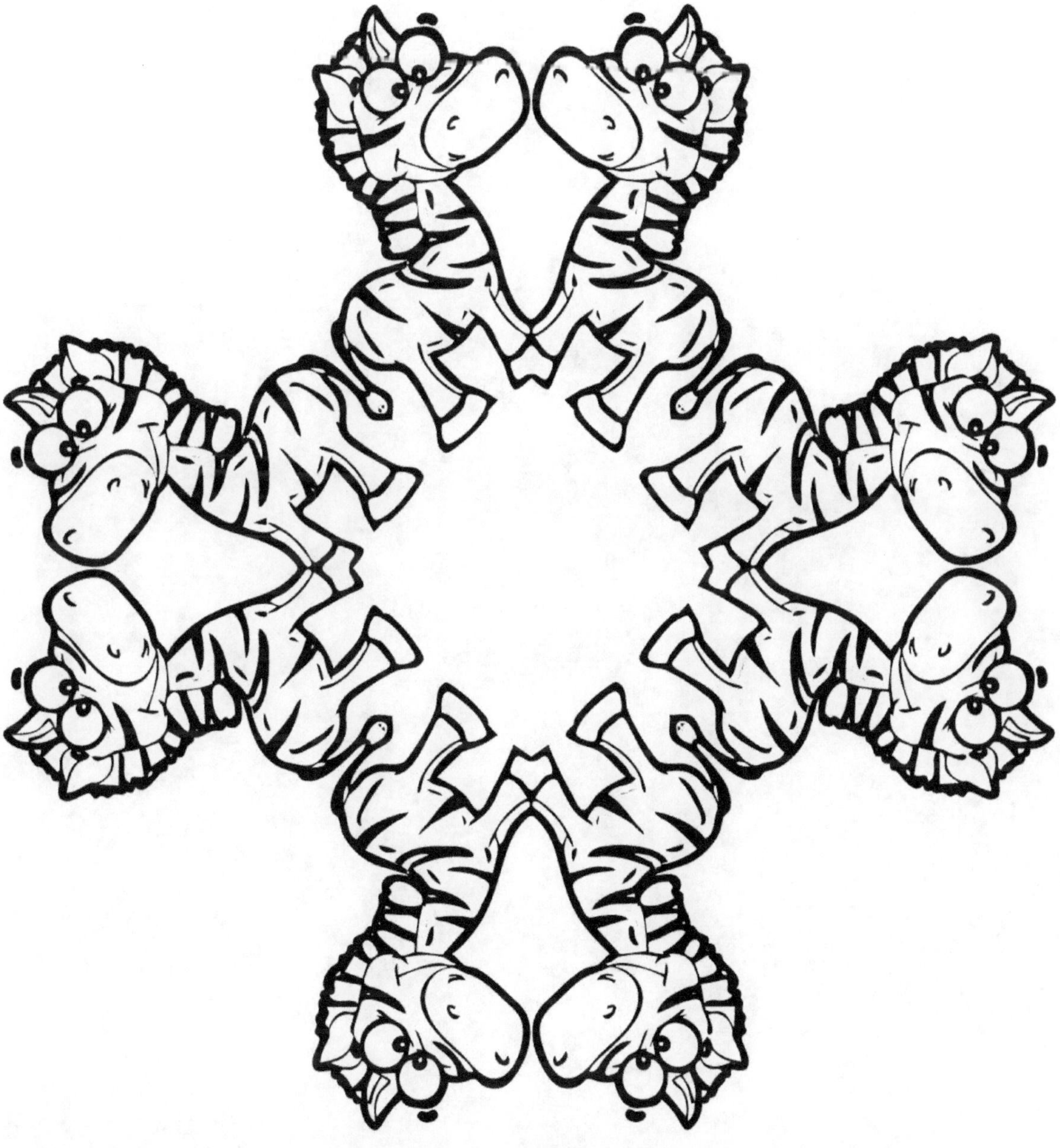

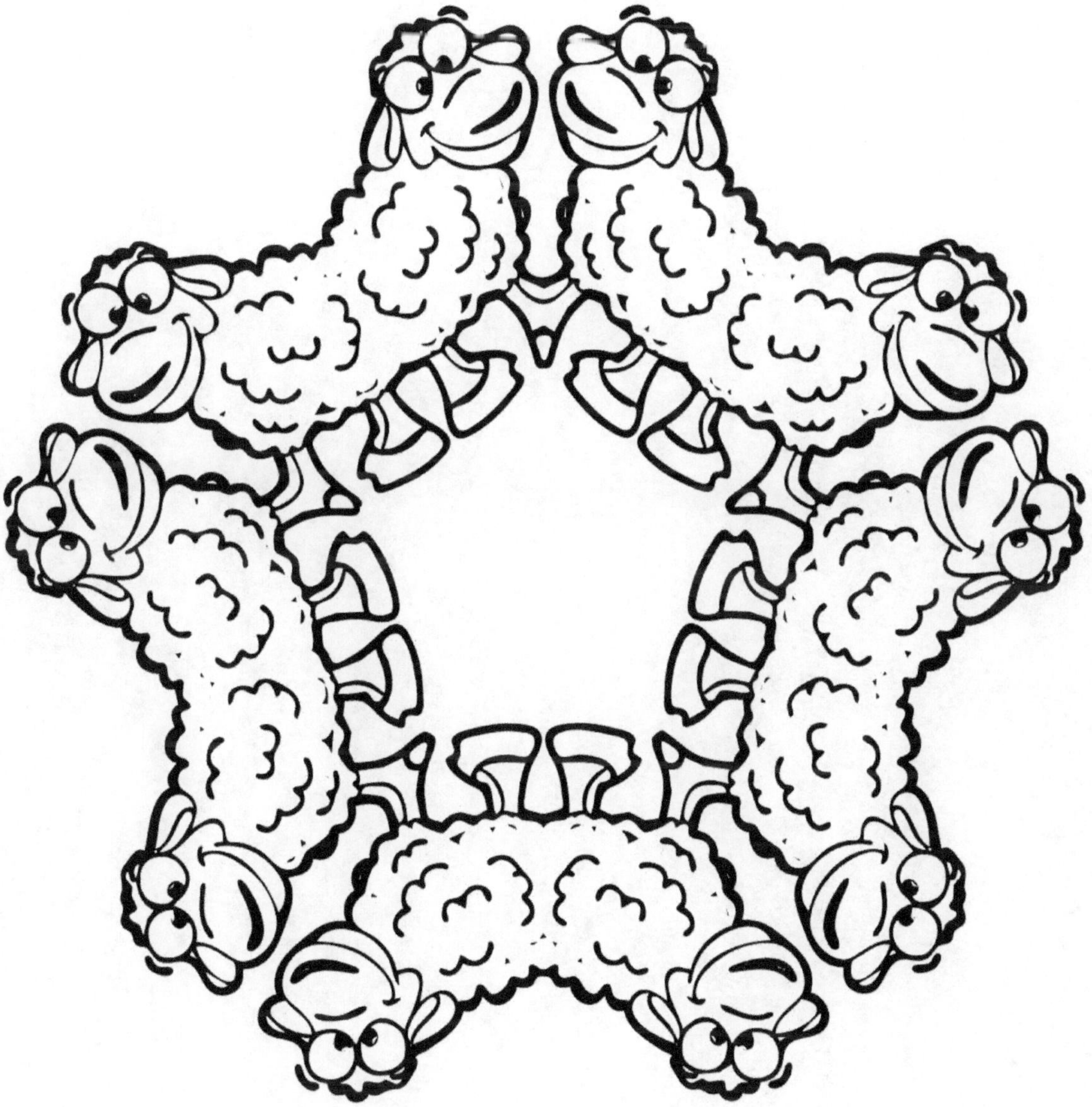

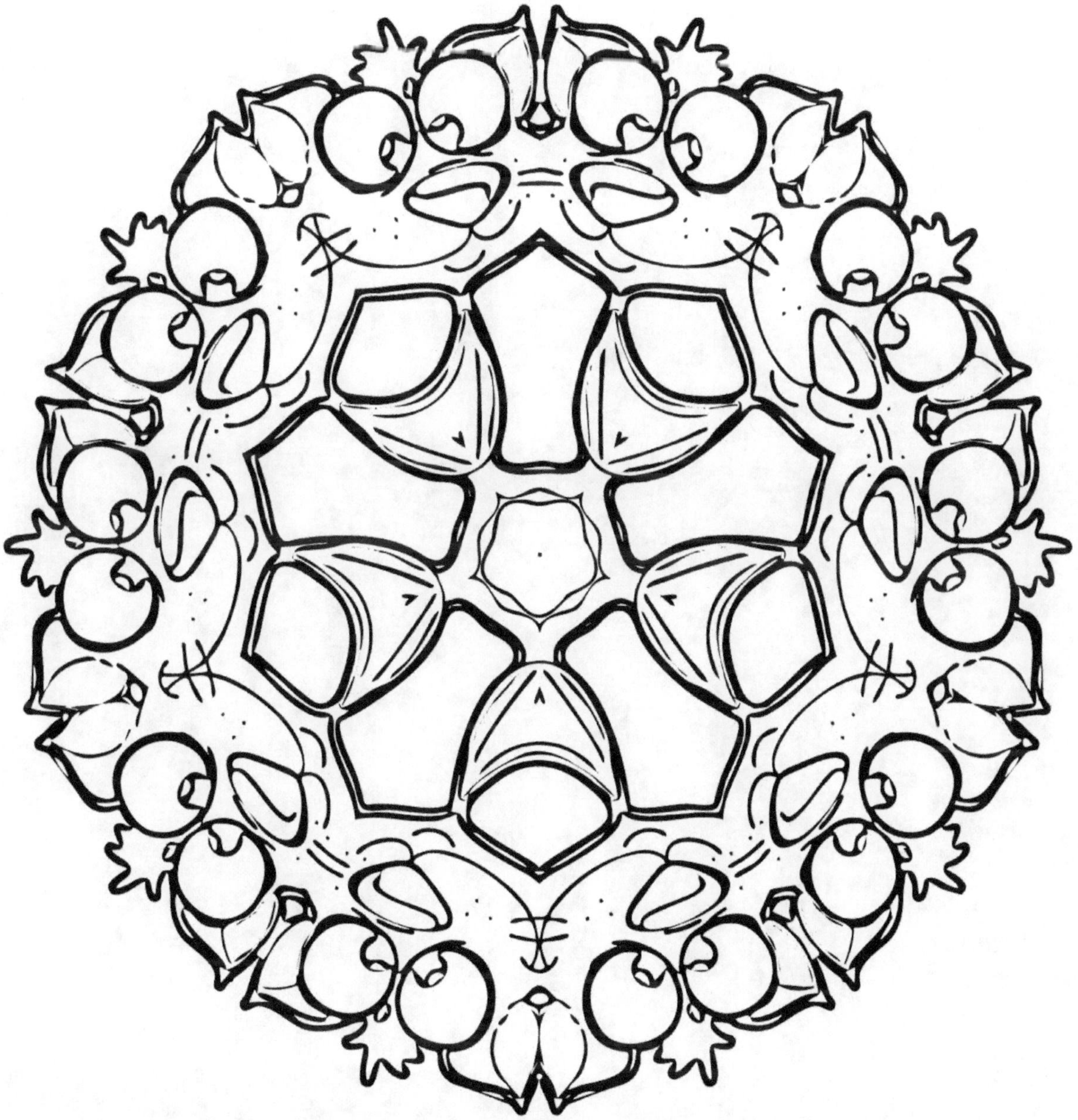

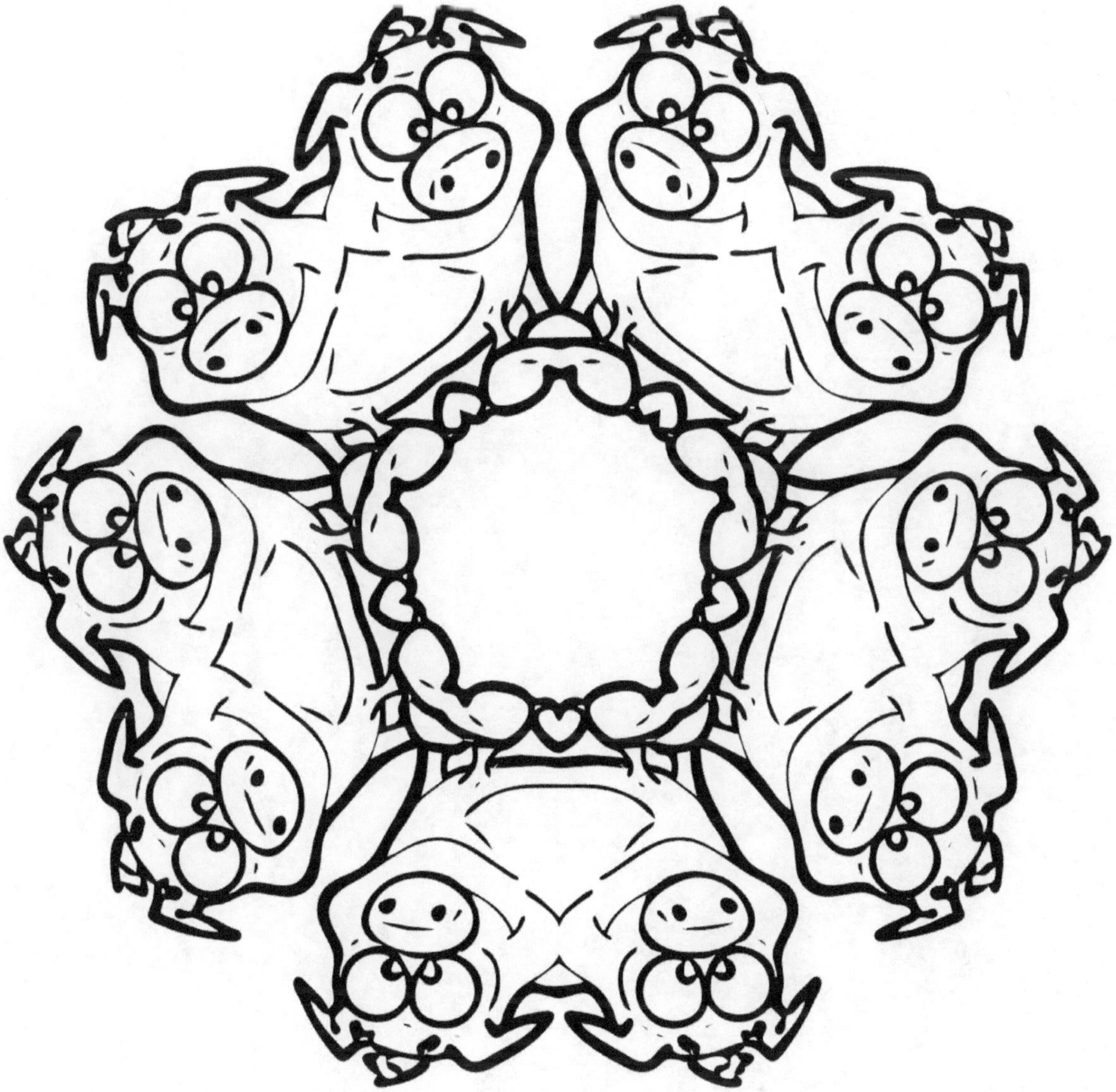

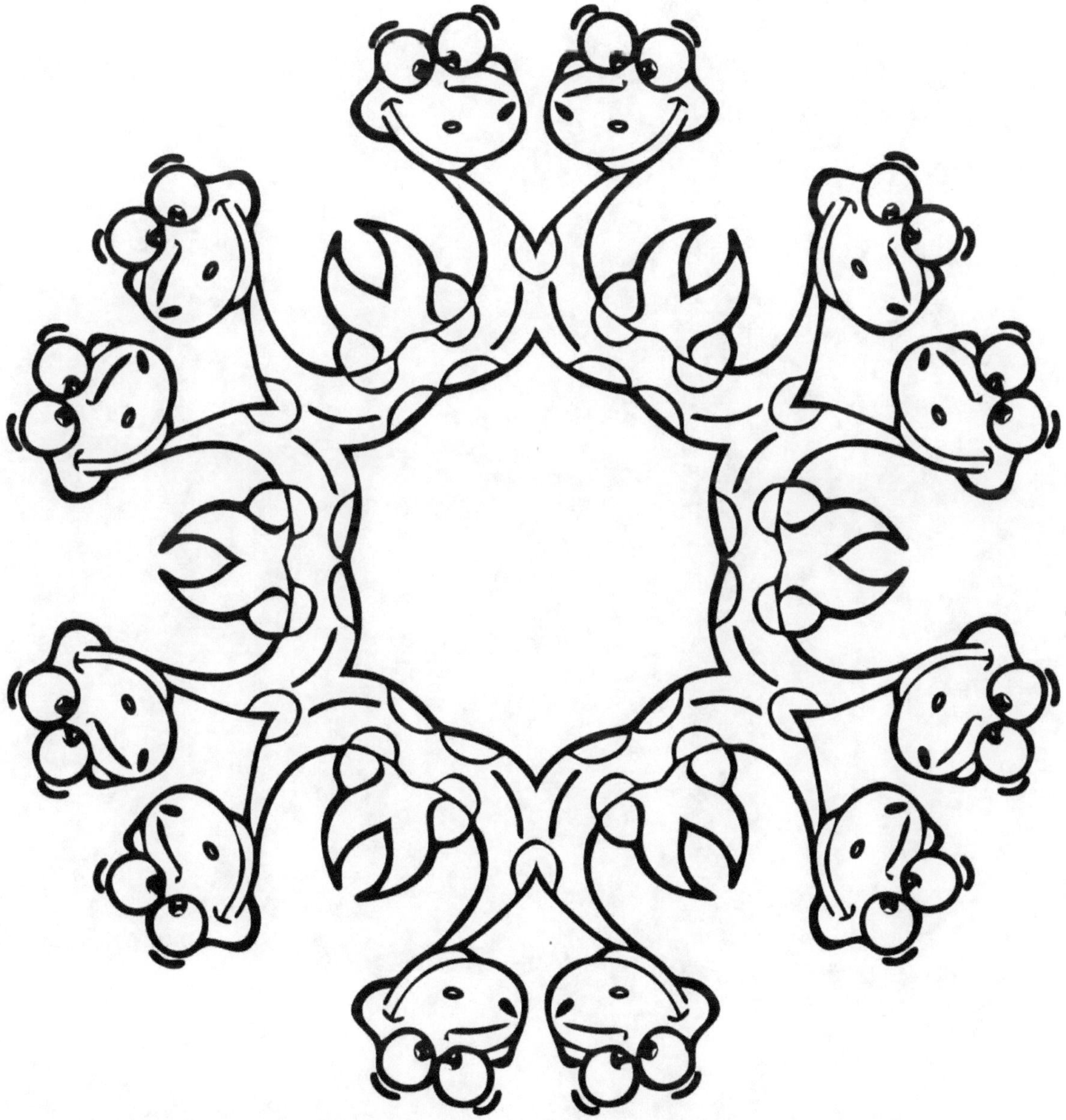

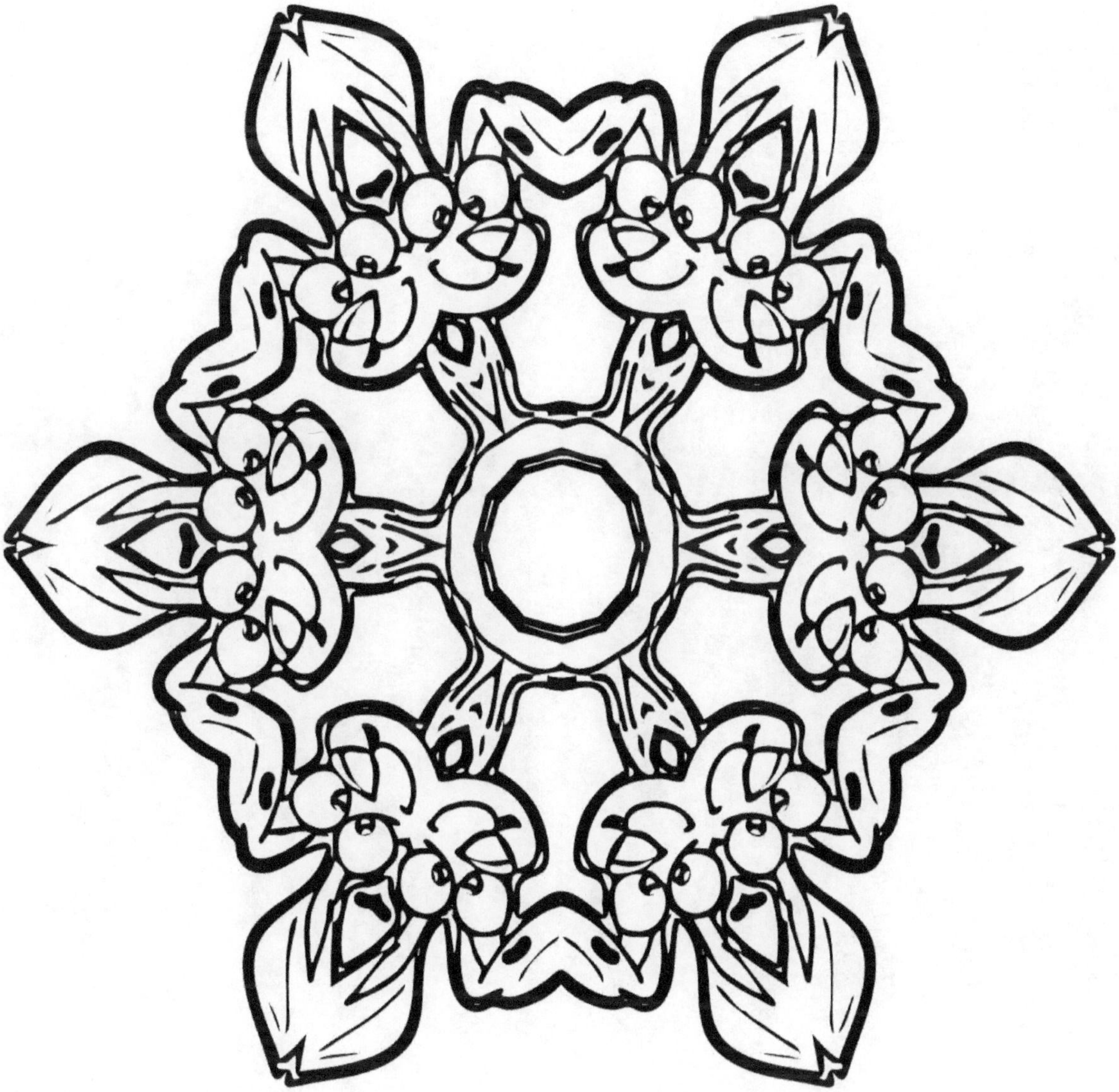

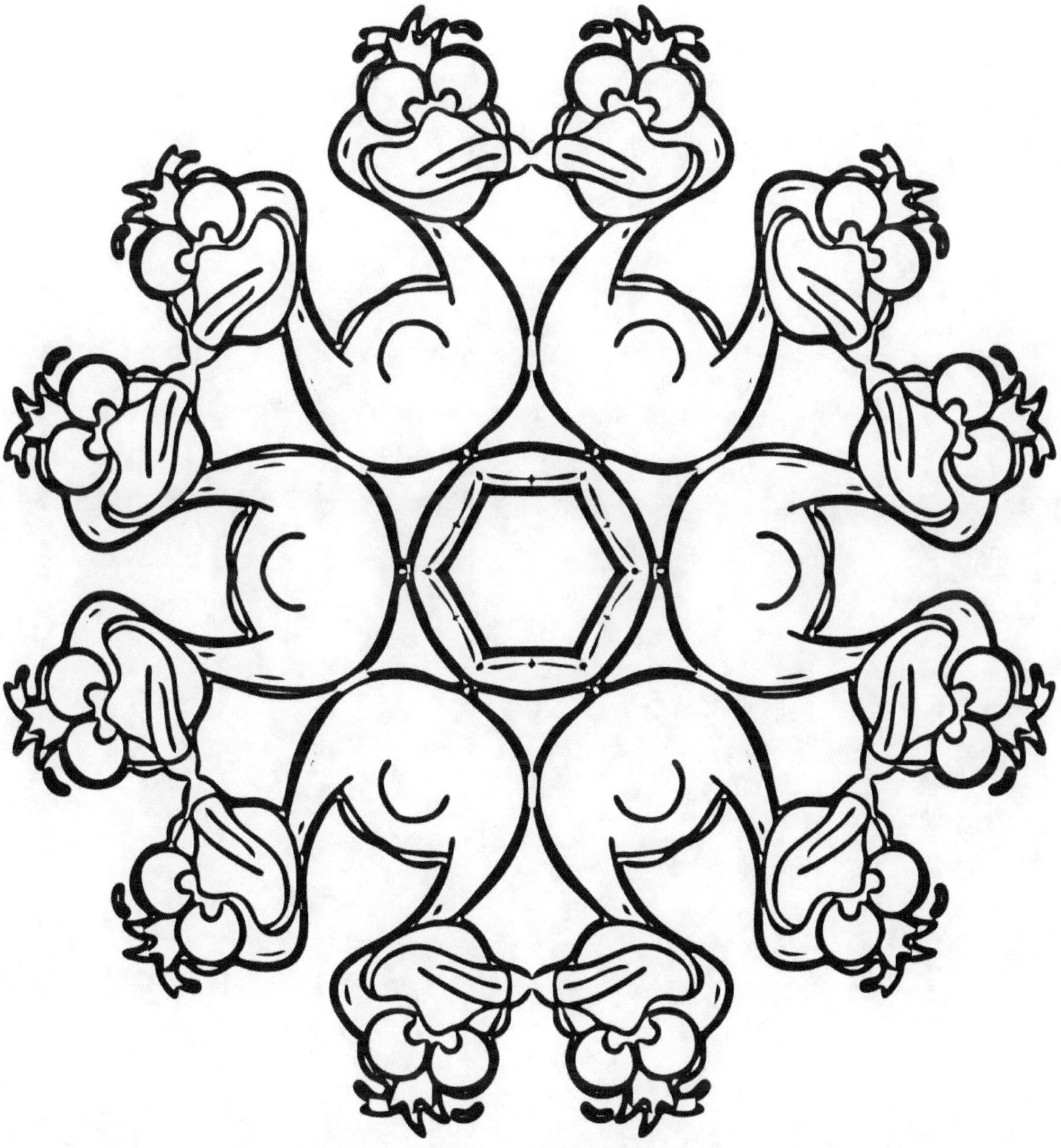

www.ingramcontent.com/pod-product-compliance
Lightning Source LLC
Chambersburg PA
CBHW080609180526
45168CB00007B/2846
* 9 7 8 1 5 1 7 7 3 1 0 1 4 *